YOU DON'T HAVE TO LIVE WITH EAR NOISES!

Do your ears ring or make other types of noise? Do you have trouble understanding people in noisy surroundings? Do you experience dizziness or loss of balance? Do you have the sensation of fullness or pressure in your ears? Do loud sounds irritate you and cause discomfort?

Any one of the above symptoms could mean that the cells of your ears are not getting the energy-supplying nutrients they need. And, contrary to popular medical wisdom, something can be done about it, no matter how old you are.

In this eye- and ear-opening booklet, Dr. Paul Yanick draws on decades of scientific research and study in the fields of biochemistry, nutrition, pharmacology, audition, immunology, gerontology, neurology, functional medicine, and Oriental medicine and lays the foundation for a whole new approach to ear health and hearing problems including tinnitus, Menière's disease, and otosclerosis.

ABOUT THE AUTHOR

Paul Yanick, Jr., Ph.D. is a world renowned authority in Bioenergetic Medicine and Quantum Nutrition. The author of several academic textbooks and over 120 scientific and clinical studies and articles, Dr. Yanick has pioneered many multidisciplinary innovations involving the relationship between nutrition, human physiology and the human energy system. His textbook, *Clinical Chemistry and Nutrition: A Physician's Reference* is widely used by doctors and universities across America.

Dr. Yanick has over 22 years of clinical experience with functional medicine and has directed hundreds of educational seminars for doctors. He is a professional member of the Internatonal Academy of Preventive Medicine, the American Bioenergetic Association, the International Society of Functional Medicine, and the International Academy of Holistic Health and Medicine.

NATURAL RELIEF FROM TINNITUS

LATEST DISCOVERIES IN THE BIOCHEMISTRY OF HEARING— NEW HELP FOR EAR PROBLEMS

by Paul Yanick, Jr., Ph.D.

Keats Publishing, Inc.  New Canaan, Connecticut

IMPORTANT NOTE
If you have a hearing loss or any other type of hearing problem, you should consult with a medical specialist (otologist). This book is not meant to replace a medical exam, nor is it meant to diagnose or render medical advice. Its intent is solely informational and educational.

NATURAL RELIEF FROM TINNITUS AND OTHER EAR DISORDERS

13 DIG/DIG 12

Contents

INTRODUCTION

Hearing is a complex miracle of mechanical, hydraulic, and electrochemical energy conversion systems that is more sophisticated than any space age electronic device or computer. Our ears monitor the world around us for sound while simultaneously maintaining our balance and informing us of our body's relative position (straight, leaning or horizontal). The neural and electrical circuits supplying this tiny but highly efficient system are extremely complex and represent the microscopic equivalent to the telephone service of a large city.

Unfortunately, however, our environment contains many threats to hearing—noise, drugs, pollutants, radiation and poor dietary nourishment. The roar of city traffic, the cacophony of an airport, and the background noise of many social situations are all major stress factors that diminish hearing ability.

Ask yourself these questions: Do you have difficulty understanding people in noisy surroundings? Do your ears ring or make other types of noise? Do you experience intermittent dizziness or loss of balance? Do you have the sensation of fullness or pressure in your ears? Do loud sounds irritate you and cause discomfort? Any one or more of the above signs and symptoms could indicate that the cells of your ear are suffering from a lack of energy-supplying nutrients.

Are you sick and tired of hearing "learn to live with these conditions" or "nothing can be done"? You *can* overcome these hearing disorders! Age need be no barrier. The capacity of our bodies to generate energy remains intact. Discover how to supply the correct types of nutrients to fuel or release this energy.

The guidelines detailed in this book have proven successful for thousands of people with ear disorders. This comprehensive, yet direct authoritative guidebook describes a simple, effective way to overcome many types of ear-related problems.

Aging Need Not Entail Hearing Loss

Many doctors maintain that nerves are damaged and ear disorders are hopeless, progressive and incurable. Doctors blame ear disorders on the aging process—but ear disorders can be overcome.

Many are led to believe that they should expect to lose their hearing as they get older. There are many civilizations in the world where people live well past 115 years of age without losing their hearing or experiencing the agony of ear noises. In fact, statistics show that more than half the hearing impaired population is not elderly, but middle-aged.

The rate and manner at which aging occurs is influenced by life events, genetic predisposition, acute and chronic illness, stress, dietary factors and the amount of physical activity. Age-related changes occur in the vital organs, including the heart, lungs, kidneys and liver. In addition, most hearing deficits are due to accelerated aging. However, this accelerated aging is related to an acidic pH and nutritional deficiencies. By engaging in regular physical activity and following the dietary guidelines in this guidebook, accelerated aging can be prevented.

Hearing Loss is Not Solely Genetic

Contrary to the idea that often prevails, ear disease itself is seldom caused solely by heredity. Genetic weaknesses can predispose individuals to auditory mechanisms highly vulnerable to stress from poor diet and environmental factors. Many of these environmental and dietary triggering agents that attack the hearing mechanism can be eliminated or decreased early in an individual's life, reducing the individual's susceptibility to ear disorders. Genetic weaknesses can also predispose individuals to have smaller, less efficient endocrine glands, organs and circulatory systems, and different digestion and absorption capabilities, which can aggravate or cause progressive hearing loss. Furthermore, many individuals inherit long-term deficiencies and biochemical imbalances that end up causing many types of hearing problems. In other words, instead of inheriting the disease or specific type of ear malfunction, certain individuals may inherit the *deficiency* that causes the ear to malfunction.

The association of the ear to the health of the entire body is often disregarded, even though the biochemical basis of disease and dysfunction apply to the ear as well. The sensory cells of the inner ear, like all living cells in our bodies, need not only water, oxygen, and a suitable ambient temperature, but a combination of over 40 nutrients. The cells of the ear will ultimately get from the blood only those nutrient elements furnished by our daily intake of food. Because nutrient needs, enzyme patterns, biochemistry, anatomy and blood circulation, and types of hearing dysfunction vary from person to person, successful nutritional support must be derived from organic-enzymatic complexes of nutrients. Ideally, each person must be evaluated as a whole unique person with diet, nutrition, exercise and relaxation programs designed to meet his or her specific needs.

Since nutrients act as a team and the cells in the ear depend upon the total spectrum of nutrients, scarcity and/or excess of even one single nutrient can reduce the efficiency of all the nutrients with which it is teamed. All nutrients are essential links in the total collection of nutrients needed by the cells of the ear and must be present in enzymatic forms to be effectively used by the body.

Many scientists believe they have found a common underlying enzyme depletion that is linked to many health conditions. Research in biochemistry, nutrition, immunology, gerontology, pathology, neurology, functional medicine and Oriental medicine is providing clues as to why different organs of the body age and malfunction—and how we can slow down these processes. Findings in these many disparate fields are laying the foundation for a whole new approach to disease prevention. They also provide the tools necessary to help prevent many ear-related disorders while stopping or slowing the progressive nature of these ear problems.

UNDERSTANDING THE EAR-BODY CONNECTION

Chirping, roaring, hissing and whistling are some of the sounds that constitute ear noise. Although it affects almost 40 million Americans, tinnitus has received little publicity. Some conditions are as extreme as the rumble of a subway car, or the roar of a jet plane.

Alcoholism, drug problems and other life-disrupting practices may occur when an afflicted individual becomes convinced his or her condition is hopeless. And it's easy to see why. We can adjust to many difficulties in life. Chronic illness is relieved by medical attention; personal relationship problems may heal in time. But continuous or intermittent bursts of noise in the ear can destroy a person's lifestyle almost overnight.

Understanding the world of a person with tinnitus requires that a person with normal hearing imagine living with noise over which there is no control; no quiet haven, only the agony of ongoing noise. Most available strategies fail to provide relief. The most common suggested remedy is "learning to live with it." This advice translates into a daily regimen of discomfort and tension for those beset by tinnitus.

For people suffering from progressive hearing loss, the most common prognosis is the same: "Learn to live with it." An invisible and insidious process, hearing loss usually begins unnoticed and escalates into a destructive force that ruins lives and careers, creates misunderstandings between friends and loved ones, causes anxiety, stress and isolation.

Many people with progressive hearing loss also complain of fullness or ear pressure sensations in the ear, loudness sensitivity or difficulty understanding people when noise or other voices are present in the background. Others suffer from dizziness, balance problems and ear noises.

Ear specialists are unable to penetrate and visually examine the hearing organ or inner ear. The inner ear's microscopic size and inaccessible location make it virtually impossible for them to perform surgery or to observe the effects of drugs on the human ear. As a result, doctors shrug their shoulders and continually give people the same "learn to live with it" advice.

MY OWN HEARING STORY

The picture need not be so bleak or pessimistic. There is an alternative, which my own personal story illustrates. When I was 19, I was a young man looking forward to college and a career in audiology. After years of taking cortisone and antibiotics for allergies and asthma, my ears ruptured and I lost a significant amount of my hearing. Unless you've experienced hearing loss, it is difficult to understand the special terror it can cause.

Within two years, I had lost 90 percent of my hearing, and was troubled by constant ear noises. Specialists from one end of the country to the other labeled my condition nerve deafness and tinnitus. They told me I would eventually go deaf and there was little they could do for me. By the time I was 20 years old I had lost all my hearing and the ear noises had increased, causing severe insomnia and anxiety. Time and time again I was given the same advice: I should adjust to the fact I would live out the rest of my life with deafness and endless ear noises.

Then a friend who was an ear specialist suggested I travel to the most advanced ear clinic in the world. After a week of many specialized hearing, blood and radiologic exams, a leading ear specialist diagnosed fatal kidney disease as the cause of my deafness. He sent me home with no hope for a cure and only one year to live.

Being tenacious, I refused to allow my life to be so drastically altered without putting up a fight. I was distressed but not defeated. I decided that if no help was available, I would devote my scholastic efforts to unraveling the mystery of hearing disorders. In short, I began to investigate my own condition.

My first step was to analyze mineral, nutrient and vitamin relationships in my own body. I suspected that, based on both the complexity of the ear and its functions, the cause of hearing loss would lie within the relationship of nutrition to health. I spent thousands of dollars on traditional blood tests that failed to reveal any imbalances in my blood chemistry. Hair analysis revealed mercury and lead toxicity and severe deficiencies of zinc, manganese and magnesium. But, repeated testing of my hair samples revealed inconsistent and unreliable information. Then, after over a year of searching for meaningful clues to my hearing loss, I discovered that the pH or acid/alkaline balance of my body was severely deranged.

My body was very acidic from eating too much animal protein and the prescription drugs I took for asthma and allergies. Using very accurate pH paper, I assessed my salivary and urine pH on different types of diets. Popular nutritionists of the 70s kept insisting that a high protein diet was best as it would prevent the low blood sugar reactions I seemed to be suffering from. In fact, two physicians diagnosed hypoglycemia and suggested a regime of megavitamins. However, when I ate a diet high in animal protein and low in carbohydrates and vegetables, my early morning pH readings became more acidic.

Therefore, I decided to experiment with a total vegetarian diet. On the vegetarian diet, I saw a very slow, but progressive improvement in my first morning urinary and saliva pH. Despite these small improvements in my pH, my ear symptoms remained the same. Could it be the megavitamins? I wondered. I stopped the megavitamins and took only whole food supplements like spirulina, green barley, bee pollen and fresh raw carrot juice. After only one week of this program, I was able to detect significant improvements in my hearing and overall health. Later, I discovered that the megavitamins were mostly synthetic and inorganic, even though they were labeled "natural." For the next eight weeks, the improvements in hearing and pH continued until I regained about 40 percent of my hearing. The ear noises decreased dramatically but were still bothersome at night when I tried to fall asleep. Now 24 years old, I was encouraged enough by my own hearing improvements to pursue further research connecting nutrition to hearing deficits—an unexplored area of medical science.

After several years of research with different whole food supplements, at 28 years old, I discovered a formula of whole foods that really made a difference. I also discovered that I had barley and bee pollen allergies and formulated my new product without green barley or bee pollen. Because of my many food allergies and weak digestive system, I designed a formula that was easy to digest and that would result in superior absorption into the cells of my body. Several years later, I also developed a process of reducing the nutrients to the smallest possible particle size so that they could reach the cells within seconds after digestion. In addition, I energized these small particles with a proprietary electromagnetic process in order to synchronize and increase enzyme activity and balance acupuncture meridians. The synchronized enzyme activity allows nutrients to be delivered more quickly and efficiently into the living cell.

Several months later, I made further improvements in the formula by combining the nutrients with phosphatidylcholine. A component of lecithin, phosphatidylcholine occurs naturally in the cell membranes throughout the body. Phosphatidylcholine enhances nutrient delivery to nerve cells. It also helps to emulsify the fat soluble nutrients in the formula, creating smaller molecules for better absorption into nerve cells.

In the 70s, many scientists and physicians referred to the inner ear as the most energy-hungry organ of the body. Thus, nutrition must play a larger role in hearing than previously suspected. After all, the body has available to it only the energy we put into it as food. Nature didn't give us the ability to manufacture energy. We are, biologically, consumers.

After dietary and lifestyle changes and supplementation with my new synchronized whole food complex blended in fresh grapefruit juice, I noticed dramatic hearing improvements as well as relief from the noise that filled my head both day and night. For the first time in years, I was able to understand speech without depending on lip reading. Speech was clear and intelligible. Hearing tests documented almost a 70 percent improvement in my speech-understanding ability.

SENSORINEURAL HEARING LOSS: NERVE DEAFNESS

The most common form of hearing loss is known as sensorineural hearing loss or nerve deafness. In most of these cases, the problem is in the sensory organ called the cochlea where highly specialized hair cells convert sounds into electrochemical energy that is sent off to the brain as nerve impulses.

The most common type of communication problem with sensorineural hearing loss is the constant reduction in the intelligibility level of the speech which is being received by the outer ear. The sensorineural patient never hears a meaningful pattern of speech that will enable him to react in an appropriate and positive fashion. The loudness and pitch of a person's voice level or background noise interference can also interfere with the speech signal. Background noise has the effect of masking, blotting out, or interfering with the higher frequency consonant sounds that give speech its clarity and intelligibility.

Most people with sensorineural hearing loss also have tinnitus and an exaggerated sensitivity to loud sounds. This sensitivity to loud sounds is known as recruitment. Many have consulted with a succession of ear specialists, groping for relief that never seems to materialize.

My quest to determine what imbalances lead to nerve-generated disorders of the inner ear has led me into many different fields of scientific study. First, realizing that the ear is the most energy hungry organ of the body, I tried to improve the quality and quantity of nutrients and whole food that I consumed. Second, the electrochemical changes that take place in the ear are critically dependent on an alkaline cellular pH. I also learned that the mineral elements sodium and potassium play a role. These occur in specific ratios with other minerals; in order to maintain optimum transmission to the brain, these ratios must be maintained.

Third, sodium and potassium exchange also takes place when the auditory nerve is stimulated, and if the smallest change occurs in the ratio between these two elements, hearing is affected. Finally, the blood flow and supply of nutrients via the small capillaries of the ear is restricted when large amounts of alcohol, caffeine and other processed and refined food ingredients are present. It became abundantly clear that nutrition plays a critical role in the proper functioning of the ear.

For the past two decades, I have helped thousands of individuals by recommending changes in their eating habits and lifestyle. Improvements with this program range from halting further hearing loss in progressive ear degeneration to dramatic improvements and nearly complete restoration of hearing ability.

By focusing on the latest research in stress control, nutrition, and exercise, this book will provide clear guidance to readers in the application of these principles to virtually any form of hearing problem. Tinnitus (ear noises), Menière's disorder (a hearing disorder accompanied by dizziness, nausea), presbycusis (hearing loss due to aging), otosclerosis (a bone disorder affecting the tiny bones and joints in the middle ear), childhood and adult ear infections, eustachian tube malfunction, fullness or pressure in the ear, sensitivity to loudness, and unclear speech perception—any one of these ailments can benefit from this approach.

TINNITUS: NOISE GENERATION OF THE INNER EAR

Imagine the constant explosion of a construction crew's jackhammer that doesn't stop at the end of the day, or the thunder of a jet taking off with a roaring echo that never fades. Imagine the sound of a hundred telephones ringing as one, or the never-ending buzz of an insect in your ear.

These are some of the nerve-wracking sounds heard by millions diagnosed as suffering from tinnitus. Tinnitus is a chronic malady, affecting one or both ears and striking men and women at any age. Over seven million Americans suffer from the nightmare of constant tinnitus. They commonly suffer from frustration, anxiety, insomnia, addictions to tranquilizers, and even alcoholism.

The causes of tinnitus are many and varied. In many cases, tinnitus increases after smoking or drinking excessive caffeine or alcohol. Other cases of tinnitus occur after antibiotic or other drug therapies, while still others seem to start after periods of excessive stress or a traumatic life event. But by far, the most common causes of tinnitus are lymph and liver toxicity, biochemical imbalances caused by diet, drugs and stress, and digestive disorders.

Traditionally, tinnitus has been treated with electronic sound "maskers" or prescription drugs designed to relax the nervous system or lower blood pressure. However, many of these drugs disrupt the body's biochemical balance and metabolism. Sound maskers are hearing aid devices that, in effect, overstimulate the ear to encourage a desensitization. However, maskers overstress, or further damage already damaged ears.

With no drug or surgery available to correct the majority of tinnitus conditions, most physicians advise patients to learn to live with their disorder.

THE BIOCHEMICAL BASIS OF TINNITUS

In order to understand why the ear can generate tinnitus, let us examine the anatomy of the inner ear in all its complex mechanical, hydraulic, and electrochemical connections to the human body. The magic of hearing lies in the way sound waves, from voice, music or noise, are funneled through the external ear to the eardrum. From the eardrum, these sound waves pass through the bone and air (*mechanical*) to be carried by fluid (*hydraulic*), which stirs microscopic hair cells that convert the waves into electrochemical impulses (*electrochemical*). Every second of every day, the hair cells of the inner ear are amplifying weak external signals so that we can hear them. When the hair cells and their neural connections lack certain nutrients they produce continuous noises—some that are like feedback from a microphone.

Hearing is possible because sound enters the ear as vibrations. These vibrations set small bones in motion that in turn cause a series of chemical reactions. These reactions are dependent upon balanced nutrition in the inner ear fluids. The inner ear produces electrical impulses which are sent to the brain, and the result is hearing. All parts of the ear demand high quantities of energy-producing nutrients in order to effectively deliver full electrical sound information to the brain. Partial or incomplete nutrient delivery can short circuit the ear's electrical energy with resultant ear noises and other hearing difficulties.

Nowhere in our body do nutritional deficiencies create more negative results than in our ears. Lined with supersensitive cells and sacs containing fluids, the ear is a wonder of chemical, mechanical and electrical engineering. Nerve cells are bathed in body fluids that require an elaborate balance of electrical charges inside and outside to function properly. This electrical charge balance does several things. The balance permits the nerves to transmit or "fire" a signal and be ready in a millisecond to fire again. When the charges around the nerve cells aren't correctly balanced, there can be unwanted firings. The result is tinnitus.

Electrical stability of the ionic concentrations within each fluid compartment of the inner ear is dependent upon adequate blood circulation, osmosis, proper drainage and absorption of its fluid through the lymphatic system of the body, and a complete and balanced nutrient delivery.

In patients with ear noises, a nutritional imbalance extends itself throughout the whole body and often escapes proper detection. The ear is affected in some individuals because it is genetically or environmentally weaker than other parts of the body.

Osmosis is a vital physiological function and is particularly indispensable in keeping a normal balance of water between the cells and the extracellular fluids. The relationship between sodium found mostly in the extracellular fluids (EFC) and potassium, which is primarily found in the intracellular fluids (IFC), permits many substances and nutrients to pass back and forth between the cells and their surrounding fluids. All living cells of semipermeable membranes depend upon osmosis for much of their activity.

The relationship of sodium or potassium to other minerals also must be assessed. Their relationship in isolation is of limited importance when we realize how other minerals can raise or lower their levels depending on whether there is a deficiency or an excess of a given mineral. It is during this sensitive process of complex interactions between the ear's mechanical components and chemical electrical circuitry that nutrition plays its important role in hearing.

Hearing happens because millions of chemical reactions take place each second in the specialized hair cells. Our biochemistry requires that electrons be transferred from molecule to molecule to change the mechanical vibrations of sound waves impinging upon the eardrum to complex electrical wave patterns that the brain perceives as meaningful information.

All these chemical reactions of the cells involve oxygen and tiny electron processors or energy generators called mitochondria. There are over 100,000 mitochondria in each cell of the body. Energy reactions in each mitochondrium depend on a sequence of enzymes that pass electrons down from one to the next. This process is called the electron transport chain (ETC). Like a waterfall turning a turbine to create electricity, the ETC causes changes in electrons that cause glucose molecules to convert into high energy compounds like adenosine triphosphate (ATP).

When a molecule loses an electron, this process is called oxidation. The process of reduction occurs when molecules gain an electron. Trillions of living cells are continually being oxidized and reduced to maintain the electrical stability of body cells.

When a molecule loses too many electrons in oxidation, it becomes unstable and begins stealing electrons from other molecules in the mitochondria. These unstable molecules are called free radicals. The stealing of electrons from other molecules creates serious electrical disturbances in the inner ear. It sets off a series of volatile chain reactions that cause great harm to cells, tissues and organs of the body.

Chemical pollutants in our air, water and food catalyze the release of free radicals in the body. Chronic emotional stress also causes an excess production of free radicals. In the healthy body, a continual tug-of-war takes place between free radicals and antioxidant enzymes. These specialized enzymes prevent an overpopulation of harmful free radicals. A lack of these protective enzymes (or a deactivation of them due to an acidic pH in the body) can cause damage to genetically weaker cells in the ear.

The body's antioxidant defense system neutralizes free radicals and employs special enzymes that serve as quencher molecules to break free radical chains and preserve the integrity of the electron transport chain. Enzymes are the first line of defense and need to be supplemented in a balanced and synchronized form to prevent damage to the specialized cells of the ear.

The chemical complexity of nerve cells and their intricate molecular milieu nurture cells that enable us to hear and experience the many beautiful sounds of nature, the human voice and musical instruments. These molecules must maintain a delicate balance for nerve cells to function properly. Even a slight disturbance in the equilibrium of enzymes, chemical messengers, charged compounds or free radicals, and calcium, can lead to the death of a specialized "hair" or nerve cell.

The active inhibitor of the otoacoustic emissions from the ear is a chemical messenger called acetylcholine. This chemical messenger travels to a nerve receptor site which consists of five proteins arranged in the shape of a flower. The proteins enclose a central channel that penetrates the core of flower-shaped receptor sites. When an acetylcholine molecule binds to two of these proteins, the channel opens for a thousandth of a second—like a camera shutter. In that instant 10,000 positively charged sodium ions rush through the channel into the nerve cell, changing its electrical state and prompting sound to be transmitted to the brain for interpretation. The efficiency of this receptor action determines the fidelity of sound transmission along the nerve pathway. A defective acetylcholine receptor, the cause of many ear problems, can be caused by:

1. A deficiency in one or more amino acids that distort the acetylcholine receptors;
2. A deficiency of choline, phospholipids and fatty acids;
3. A deficiency or imbalance of mineral elements or electrically charged mineral elements;
4. A toxic overload of nerve cells and receptor sites that block the flow of ions along nerve pathways;
5. Disturbed energetic pathways (meridians) that can electromagnetically cause biochemical imbalances and blockages in the flow of electrons along nerve pathways.

The field of bioenergetic medicine—in which scientists emulate nature's own processes for fashioning high-quality energy compounds—is emerging with force. Increasingly, doctors in Europe are turning to the field of energy medicine for innovative ideas about how to make nerve cells electrically active and physically resilient.

When one or more of the above deficits exist, hair cells become deprived of oxygen and go into states of exhaustion. These oxygen-deprived cells no longer have the energy to close calcium channels, as they are supposed to once a nerve signal is transmitted. Too much calcium flows into the cells, disturbing electrical equilibrium and eventually causing the hair cells to die. Before these cells die, they send disturbed electrical signals called tinnitus.

The Role of Nutrition

What, then, can nutritional biochemistry contribute to this deficit in sound transmission? Over the past twenty years, neuroscientists have made considerable strides in understanding the workings of the inner ear. Can science explain how and why tinnitus is generated? The simple answer is no. There is, as yet, no proper understanding of what happens in the inner ear when sound distortions are generated. However, existing research in many other scientific disciplines can provide insights into the biochemistry of the hearing process and how it can be altered by deficits in critical nerve nutrients.

At first I thought these deficits were alike and due to the same deficiency states. After over two decades of research, I made a discovery that revolutionized my thinking about the electrochemical process of hearing: The pH (acid or alkaline balance) was acidic in all patients with ear disorders and the acid pH suppressed enzyme activity, causing the enzymatic complexes of mineral elements to become electrically unstable. My research provided a biological framework for examining dysfunctions of the ear. In fact, animal studies have already confirmed my earlier clinical discoveries regarding the connection between critical nerve nutrients and ear-related distortions.

All parts of the ear demand sufficient quantities of energy-producing compounds and nutrients in order to effectively deliver high quality and complete electrical sound information to the brain. Partial or incomplete nutrient delivery can short-circuit the ear's electrical energy. The result: ear noises or other hearing problems.

Growing evidence suggests that nerve cells are particularly vulnerable to free radical damage. The myelin sheath (the fatty material that covers nerve fibers) like the mitochondria is rich in fatty acids and highly susceptible to free radical attack. Deficiencies of fatty acids and prostaglandins are common in tinnitus cases. Prostaglandins are produced within each active cell of the body in order to help the body with inflammation and to control blood pressure. Fatty acid deficiencies can cause a loss of specialized nerve cells due to free radical damage. This free radical damage causes accelerated electrical disturbances (tinnitus) and nerve degeneration (hearing and balance disorders).

Maintaining the delicate balance between antioxidant enzymes is critical for the body to dispose of free radicals before they can do any damage. Up-to-date research suggests that halting nerve cell damage can be accomplished by correcting the fundamental deficiency states of enzymes.[1-5]

The intricate cellular milieu nurtures cells that enable us to hear, see, think and perform numerous other functions. These molecules must maintain a delicate balance for nerve cells to function properly. Even a slight disturbance in the equilibrium of enzymes can lead to the death or poor performance of a sensory cell and, ultimately, the development of sensorineural-type ear disorders. An enzyme called superoxide dismutase is provided by the healthy body to protect nerve cells from damage. It is well known that free radicals cause nerve cells to die.

The common term "nerve deafness" is really a misnomer. Since the cochlea is the primary site of dysfunction, clinicians are beginning to use the term sensorineural or cochlear hearing loss. Degeneration of specialized hair and nerve connections in the cochlea are the major causes of failing hearing and distortions of the inner ear.

There are many causes and varying deficiency states found in tinnitus and sensorineural hearing loss patients. Ideally, any protocol of adjunctive nutritional support must be tailored to compensate for these deficiency states and imbalances—especially the balancing of accupoints with specific homeopathic remedies. However, most persons who suffer from this disorder may benefit from the following adjunctive nutritional support:

- **Spirulina:** a rich source of organic beta carotene, with high concentration of organic minerals, fatty acids and proteins that are alkaline and easy to assimilate into the cells.
- **Organic pumpkin seed oil or raw seeds:** a source of organic zinc, essential for the metabolism of phosphorus and protein. The inner ear has the highest concentration of zinc in the body.
- **Beta carotene:** Ideally from marine algae (duneilla); important for the structural integrity of sensory hair cells of the inner ear.
- **Chlorophyll complex:** a source of organic magnesium which plays a role in some 300 enzymatic reactions in intermediary metabolism.
- **Royal jelly:** an excellent source of organic B vitamins, especially pantothenic acid.
- **Pfaffia paniculata:** an excellent herbal tonic for strengthening immunity and balancing the body's endocrine and nervous systems.
- **Astragalus:** a strengthening tonic formula with immune enhancing properties.
- **Ginkgo biloba:** an excellent microcirculation booster and free radical inhibitor; also helps to balance electrolytes.
- **Passionflower:** a natural antispasmodic that provides calming, anti-anxiety action and fortifies the nervous system.
- **Unsaturated fatty acids:** from cold pressed and organic unrefined olive, safflower and flax oils.
- **Evening primrose oil:** a source of prostaglandins (gamma linolenic acid).
- **Choline:** critical for the metabolism and transport of fats and cholesterol; a precursor for the biosynthesis of phospholipids and the neurotransmitter acetylcholine.
- **Phosphatidylcholine:** an important contributor to blood and brain choline concentrations which help to determine the rate of acetylcholine biosynthesis, especially during rapid firing of cholinergic neurons, as in the hearing process.

- **Vitamin E:** helps to fortify nerves and strengthen capillary walls.
- **Licorice root:** anti-inflammatory action, helps to strengthen adrenals which, along with the kidneys, help to control electrolyte balance.
- **Ginger root:** activates digestive action, helps to prevent the nauseating symptoms of Menière's and may be helpful in reducing dizziness and vertigo.
- **High fiber brewer's yeast:** a source of organic B vitamins and trace minerals.
- **Taurine:** helps to keep the nerve cells in electrical balance and prevent runaway nerve impulses by allowing nerve currents to flow correctly.

The sensible use of these high-quality, organic supplements may prove beneficial to general health and well-being. However, supplements are not a substitute to following the healthy diet outlined later in this guidebook. Following the diet provides the foundation of health; supplements strengthen that foundation a little bit more.

Megavitamin abusers and those who take daily multivitamins that are synthetic (often labeled "natural") are fooling themselves if they think that these supplements can make up for not eating a good diet. People who take the adjunctive nutrients suggested in this guidebook might expect to get the same quick results that a strong drug prescribed for an illness delivers. If they don't notice the effects of diet or supplements quickly, they may give up and not take their diet seriously.

In fact, most people with tinnitus and ear-related problems will not detect any significant changes in their hearing ability overnight while on this program. Usually, the process of correcting long-term deficiency states and biochemical imbalances will take months. Be patient and you will reap the rewards. Even if the diet and supplementation fail to provide quick relief from ear problems, they will improve general health and well-being. Nutrition is about wellness, not illness. It is about improving the health and vitality of every cell in the body—including the cells of the ear that fail to perform optimally.

MENIÈRE'S DISEASE

The inner ear also contains a "gyroscope" device that maintains our balance. This is called the vestibular system. In hearing disorders like Menière's disease, the chemical imbalances of the vestibular system cause people to get dizzy and lose balance. The sensation of being unable to maintain balance is quite different from feeling lightheaded or giddy. The dizziness caused by this disorder is apt to be incapacitating.

Dizziness is a symptom of troubled stability, a disturbance of one's sense of relationship to space. Vertigo is a more severe form of dizziness but is differentiated from dizziness by the distinctive sense of motion that the sufferer has of himself or of his surroundings ("the room whirls around me"). Sometimes the room seems to be moving while the victim's eyes are open and sometimes he himself seems to be moving when his eyes are closed. Vertigo victims also suffer from nausea and vomiting, sweating and even an inability to stand.

Menière's disease is characterized by extreme dizziness, tinnitus and fullness or pressure of the inner ear. Excessive use of table salt and saturated fat seems to precipitate attacks of dizziness in the majority of patients. The disorder affects millions of Americans, usually between the ages of 40 and 60. Although hearing loss is usually limited to one ear, some cases have hearing loss and loudness sensitivity in both ears.

The human balance system—our normal positional stability— is the product of the operation of four different bodily systems in the healthy person: the inner ear's vestibular system; the eyesight and related muscles; muscles and joints of the body with their sense of position; and the electromagnetic meridian system which determines how electrical energy will flow throughout the body.

Nutritional Support

Like tinnitus and sensorineural hearing disorders, Menière's disease has many causes and, ideally, any protocol of adjunctive nutritional support must be tailored to individual needs. However, most persons who suffer from this disorder benefit from the following adjunctive nutritional support:

- **Unsaturated fatty acids:** from cold pressed and organic unrefined olive, safflower and flaxseed oils.
- **Evening primrose oil:** a source of gamma linolenic acid.
- **Chlorophyll complex:** a source of organic magnesium which plays a role in some 300 enzymatic reactions in intermediary metabolism.
- **Choline:** critical for the metabolism and transport of fats and choles-

terol and a precursor of the biosynthesis of phospholipids and the neurotransmitter acetylcholine.

- **Phosphatidylcholine:** an important contributor to blood and brain choline concentrations which help to determine the rate of acetylcholine biosynthesis, especially during rapid firing of cholinergic neurons, as in the hearing process.
- **Vitamin E:** helps to fortify nerves and strengthen capillary walls.
- **Licorice root:** anti-inflammatory action.
- **Ginger root:** activates digestive action, helps to prevent the nauseating symptoms of Menière's and may be helpful in reducing dizziness and vertigo.
- **Raw pumpkin seeds:** a source of organic zinc, essential for the metabolism of phosphorus and protein. The inner ear has the highest concentration of zinc in the body.
- **High fiber brewer's yeast:** a source of organic B vitamins and trace minerals.

SOUND TRANSMISSION DEFICITS

The gentle sound of a far-off stream, whistling bird songs, wind in the trees, beautiful music and cherished voices . . . what a treasure is our sense of hearing. Yet, millions of Americans are deprived of hearing these beautiful sounds because they have sound transmission deficits affecting the complex mechanical, hydraulic and electrochemical functions of the ear. Let us examine the function of the human ear in regard to these complex systems.

MECHANICAL SOUND TRANSMISSION: THE BONE CONNECTION

Mechanical transmission of sound vibrations through the external and middle ear causes vibrations to reach the inner ear where the sound waves are converted into electrochemical information. The outer ear, functioning as a sound collector, funnels sound into the ear canal. Sound then stimulates the eardrum to vibrate, transmitting and pushing the sound into the middle ear. The middle ear contains an intricate system of levers known as the hammer, anvil and stirrup. These three tiny bones (the smallest of any in the body) transmit the sound vibrations at a slower, less pronounced rate into the inner ear or cochlea. When these tiny bones stiffen or become less able to transmit sound vibrations, a condition commonly diagnosed as otosclerosis exists.

OTOSCLEROSIS

Otosclerosis is an abnormal condition of the middle or inner ear that interferes with the passage of sound along the ear canal to the inner ear. Any problems with the mobility of these three tiny bones can cause a hearing loss and in some cases tinnitus. In people who have this problem, audiologists find that bone conduction hearing is better than air conduction hearing. In other words, sounds vibrating directly on your skull, behind the ear, bypass the middle ear system of levers and stimulate the cochlea directly. If there is a problem with the middle ear bone structures, hearing through the normal channels (ear canal, ear drum, and bone structures) is poor.

Patients can perform this basic test using a low frequency tuning fork: While the tuning fork is buzzing, place it in front of the ear. Immediately place it in back of the ear on the mastoid bone. If the sound seems louder behind the ear, an individual should have more audiological testing to determine the exact nature of the hearing loss.

Almost all ear, nose and throat physicians agree that the term otosclerosis is a misnomer. Research has found that the bones don't harden but actually become soft and spongy. Physiologists have long known that the hardness of bone structures can be attributed to the amino acid (protein) and calcium content of the bone. Evidence shows that bone is a structure of fibrous protein which is hardened by the presence of calcium. My research on people with otosclerosis has revealed deficiencies and imbalances of amino acids, the essential fatty acids, calcium, and phosphorus in every case. Knowing the nutritional content of bone structure makes it the obvious place to look for answers. However, many physicians would prefer to perform ear surgery, cutting out and replacing the bones, than to try to find the origin of the problem.

Other physiologists and biochemists have demonstrated that the blood will draw out calcium from the bones when the diet is deficient in calcium or phosphorus. In this case, the blood will show normal calcium levels while bones are chronically deficient Radiologists are unable to detect this bone loss of calcium on x-rays until over 60 percent of the calcium is lost from the bones

If the body is too alkaline or the parasympathetic nervous system is overactive, one can take calcium but not assimilate any of it. Calcium, like iron, zinc and other acid-based minerals, needs a sufficient supply of hydrochloric acid. Studies show that adults over 50 have 80 to 90 percent less hydrochloric acid secretions than young children or teenagers. No wonder this ear condition is progressive!

Other systemic imbalances can cause problems with the assimilation of calcium. They are all related to refined and processed foods, toxic metal accumulations, and drugs. For instance, aluminum accumulations in the body destroy phosphorus which is necessary for the proper deposition of calcium in the bones. Studies show that most Americans consume 20 mg of aluminum per day. The sources of aluminum are mainly aluminum cookware, antacids, baking powder, drugs, and food additives. Some antacids contain up to 200 mg per dose. A teaspoonful of most baking powder contains up to 70 mg of aluminum.

Recently, scientists began to recognize the dangers of aluminum. It not only accumulates in the lungs, liver and lymph nodes, but it finds its way deep into bone structures. As it passes through the intestinal tract, it picks up phosphorus, rendering it inactive. It is well known that only a small intake of aluminum salts cause the body to dump large amounts of calcium via the urine.

Some doctors will prescribe sodium fluoride for otosclerosis.[6]

However, it is well known that fluoride destroys enzymes in the body. Since enzymes are critical to cellular and metabolic functions and help protect the body from free radicals, suppressing their protective activity causes further hearing loss and degeneration of the inner ear.

Lead toxicity is also a major cause of calcium loss in the body. Lead forces calcium out of the body through elimination channels. People who dye or color their hair or who live or work in a polluted environment generally have high lead levels.

My long-term clinical studies with otosclerosis reveal the following:

1. All otosclerosis cases involve an acid pH. The acidity forces calcium out of the bones of the inner ear and body, creating a bone loss of calcium. Taking calcium supplements does not improve this condition as the body will continue to take calcium from the bones in order to buffer or render harmless the high amount of acids generated by dietary and stress factors.

2. All cases are deficient in calcium and magnesium and, according to intracellular studies, have imbalances between calcium and phosphorus, calcium and magnesium, and calcium and potassium.

3. About 60 percent of these cases have mercury, lead or aluminum toxicity, as documented by hair analysis or other methods of assessment. Detoxification with a predominantly raw food diet, and individualized homeopathic medicines coupled with specific nutrients are successful in helping the body excrete these toxic minerals. In some cases, removing silver amalgam dental fillings is also necessary.

These mineral imbalances are corrected by balancing pH with a diet high in whole complex carbohydrates, vegetables and fruit. The diet also must exclude animal fats that bind calcium and block its absorption into the bone structure. Although improvement is very slow in these cases (due to permanent damage to bone structures of the middle and inner ear), the progression of deafness is halted and ear noises decrease in the majority of cases.

HYDRAULIC SOUND TRANSMISSION:
THE LYMPHATIC CONNECTION

Earlier I explained how the mechanical force transmitted by the eardrum brings sound vibrations into the inner ear. The bone and muscle connection of the middle ear acts as a piston pressing into the lymphatic fluids of the inner ear. This form of transmission by pressure allows the ears to be amazingly sensitive to a wide range of frequencies of sound.

Perhaps the greatest discovery concerns the connection of the body's lymphatic system to the ear. The cochlea contains various kinds of lymph fluid, each bearing a unique concentration of electrolytes (mineral elements). The differences in chemistry between these fluids is partly responsible for electrical generation by the cochlea. Except in Hungary and Italy, no researchers have documented how the ear interacts with the body's lymphatic system. Although the physiology of lymph circulation is too complex to describe in this booklet, the following information will help you understand its basic function.

The lymphatic system is one of the most overlooked systems of the body. In fact, very few people are actually aware of the functions of the lymphatic system and its critical importance to general health. A healthy lymphatic system will prevent many diseases in the human body. One of the major functions of the lymphatic system is to carry toxins from body cells. Waste products from cellular metabolism, excess trapped toxic residues from over ingestion of protein, mucus and other chemical toxins are transported by the lymphatic system and absorbed primarily through the walls of the colon from which they are eliminated by the body.

Lymph fluid is formed from the blood and contains white blood cells known as lymphocytes. Lymphocytes circulate in and out of the lymphatic system, and help strengthen it, thus strengthening the body's immunity by destroying bacteria, viruses and parasites. In order for the lymph fluid to flow and circulate throughout the body effectively, it must be of a watery consistency. Excess mucus present in the lymphatic system impairs lymphatic circulation causing overall general lymphatic congestion and, in acute conditions, swollen and inflamed lymph glands and fullness and pressure sensations in the ear.

When the colon is unobstructed, it will absorb lymphatic waste effectively through its walls into its interior. However, when the colon wall is obstructed by linings of old fecal matter or excess amounts of mucoid matter, its ability to dispose of waste matter is inhibited, causing a back-up of lymphatic wastes and mucoid matter into the lymphatic system of the inner ear. A diet high in mucoid forming foods, chemicals, processed, refined, cooked and fried foods will cause a plaster-like coating on the walls of the colon. These hardened fecal deposits on the colon walls cause excessive fermentation and putrefaction of food that allows large amounts of pathogenic bacteria to proliferate.

There are two distinct types of bacteria present in the colon. First, bacteria that result from putrefaction and fermentation in the colon; the most common species of this form of bacteria are known as *coliform bacteria*. The other type of bacteria found in the colon are known as *lactobacteria*. Lactobacteria are often referred to as "friendly" or healthy bacteria because they produce digestive enzymes that are necessary for the breakdown of food residues and they help synthesize and produce vitamins. Incompletely absorbed and digested, fermented and putrefactive foods alter the bacterial flora by generating large amounts of potentially harmful metabolites, organic acids and unhealthy bacteria in the colon.

The common practice of administering large quantities of lactobacteria contained in yogurt, kefir or acidophilus supplementation will not provide a solution to an unhealthy colon. Any relief provided is only temporary because the coliform bacteria greatly outnumber the lactobacteria. Also, coliform bacteria are constantly regenerated by putrefactive matter in the colon. Furthermore, these forms of lactobacteria contain excess amounts of lactic acid, a waste product of metabolism that, in severe cases, will cause stiffness and pain in the muscles and joints of the body. In addition, too much lactic acid in the colon is toxic to the lactobacteria, causing many to die.

As previously mentioned, lactobacteria in sufficient quantities are necessary for absorption, production, assimilation and utilization of vitamins, particularly the B vitamins. It is my experience that the colon must be thoroughly cleansed and nourished before proper implantation of live lactobacteria can take place in the colon. Only then will the lymphatic system of the inner ear properly excrete toxic metabolites through the lymphatic networks and out of the body through the bowels.

A high fiber diet rich in fruits, vegetables and whole grains ensures regular bowel cleansing and a healthy lymphatic system.

ELECTROCHEMICAL SOUND TRANSMISSION

The hydraulic energy and the resulting mechanical motion o the membrane must be converted into electrochemical energy Over 17,000 tiny hair cells react to the mechanical and hydrauli transmission of sound by electrochemical charges that excite nerv fibers. From the hair cells and their nerve fibers, the neural path way leads through the 30,000 nerve fibers that make up the audi tory nerves to the brain. In the perception of sound, a series o neural impulses race through the brain, which locates the sourc of sound by distinguishing time differences of a few microsecond (millionths of a second) between when these sounds strike you right and left ears. This truly awesome system can fire off signal through the nerves at a rate of one thousand messages a second But despite all this complexity, the basic building block of th nervous system—the brain, the spinal cord, the acoustic nerve an other nerves—is the neuron itself. The neuron is an amazing min iaturized chemical factory that needs 15 billion atoms of oxyge per second. A reduction in this oxygen supply due to reductio in blood supply to the inner ear can create sound distortions (ea noises) and cause hearing and balance disorders.

For the past few decades, auditory scientists have analyzed th chemical constituents of the animal cochlea or inner ear. The findings clearly indicate that the hearing process is electrochemic in nature. In other words, electrically charged ions (mineral el ments) in complex arrangements between various compartment of the cochlea allow electrical charges to be generated. In the ele trical mapping of the cochlea, they have found certain areas pos tively charged and other areas with negative charges.

Necessary Nutrients

Electrical stability of the ionic concentrations within each flui compartment of the inner ear is dependent upon an adequate i take of organic magnesium and potassium. Amino acids, vitamir functioning as co-enzymes, and fatty acids also have a direct i fluence on the electrical stability of the cochlea. The possibiliti are endless when you consider that over 300 nutrient ratios nee to be in balance for optimal electrochemical generation in the inn ear. Biochemical individuality further complicates matters. Aft evaluating thousands of patients biochemically, I have yet to fir two people with tinnitus or any similar ear disorder with the same exact pattern of imbalance.

Therefore, there is no simple, quick solution for the complex problems of the inner ear. The cochlea has a delicate and subtle balance of nutrients that must be maintained by the quality of the food we eat. Many long-term deficiencies and imbalances commonly take six to twelve months to correct themselves. This is due to the fact that many individuals have been deficient in a given nutrient most of their lives.

The source of energy for the cochlea is cellular respiration. During this process, complex foods are broken down into simpler substances which are then oxidized in the individual cells of the cochlea. Glucose, as well as other nutrients, are transformed by the action of enzymes into a series of intermediate compounds in an interlocking, step-by-step process. The direct source of energy is not glucose but the nutrients produced in these complex reactions.

Scientists have discovered that interference in biochemical mechanisms of metabolism is found at specific points where great demands for enzymes exist. It is well known that magnesium is a critical nutrient needed during several stages of the cell's energy cycles. In addition, the nutrient connection to cellular respiration is well documented in most authoritative textbooks. However, this information is not studied in any detail by students in medical school. Instead, students pursue detailed studies of toxic, pharmaceutical drugs, many of which destroy enzymes and cause severe nutrient imbalances.

Once we understand that there are thousands of enzyme-controlled reactions in the body, and only a fraction of them are performing in the manner nature dictates, we see the crucial role nutrition plays in our hearing and overall health.

THE CELLULAR CONNECTION

Now that I have discussed the basic biochemistry of ear problems, let us look at the cellular connection. The inner ear is composed of millions of specialized cells. Some basic facts regarding cellular function will help explain the role that nutrients play in the health of all the body's cells.

Physiologists have learned that over 24 billion cells break down

each day in the human body. Tissue and cell repair and replace-
ment require the following:

1. A constant, uninterrupted supply of nerve impulses;
2. A constant, uninterrupted supply of blood;
3. A constant, uninterrupted supply of electromagnetic energy through
   the acupuncture meridians;
4. A synchronized, organic form of all nutrients: vitamins, minerals,
   trace mineral activators, enzymes, co-enzymes, apoenzymes and
   amino acids;
5. A reduction of many inorganic toxins in foods and water.

Over 300 trillion red blood cells (RBCs) circulate through over
70,000 miles of blood vessels. The human body must produce 15
million RBCs per second in order to replace the over 15 million
RBCs that are dissolved or constantly breaking down. This is a
turnover of 900 million RBCs per hour that must be disposed of
and replaced. The efficiency of this incredible process depends
upon a complete chain of nutrients in the human body. For instance, hemolytic anemia can occur if only one out of 300 amino
acid residues in the linear polypeptide chain of hemoglobin is
missing.

Physiologists and biochemists have long known that all living
cells require energy from a selection of over 40 nutrients. Whole
nourishment to brain cells, retinal cells, cochlear cells, heart cells,
digestive cells, and kidney cells will make the processes of thinking, seeing, digesting, hearing, pumping of blood, and elimination
of waste products take place more effectively.

THE CIRCULATORY CONNECTION

The internal auditory artery is the main source of blood supply
to the human inner ear. It is important to note, however, that from
person to person, tremendous variations exist in the size, length,
course and branching out of this vessel as one part goes to the
cochlea and the other supplies the balance mechanism. This ana-
tomical fact provides a reasonable and sound explanation of why
not all malnourished people suffer from ear disorders. Those with
smaller, less efficient circulatory systems will have ears that are

more susceptible to malfunctions or damage due to stress, noise, malnourishment, or a buildup of toxins.

Ample evidence by ear specialists themselves demonstrates that many cochlear problems are due to metabolic imbalances. Studies show that a reduction in animal fat and cholesterol is necessary to increase blood flow to the inner ear.[9-18] Dr. J.T. Spencer, a West Virginia physician, found that elevated blood fats can cause ear disorders such as tinnitus and hearing loss. After dietary changes, he has reported tinnitus relief and hearing improvements in hundreds of patients.[14-17] Many auditory scientists have clearly demonstrated that any interference with blood flow to the cochlea produces damage to the hair cells. Dr. S. Rosen, a New York City physician, found a high incidence of cochlear hearing problems in people with arteriosclerosis.[18]

Initiated by free radicals and poor dietary choices, arteriosclerosis is the result of changes in the walls of the arteries, leading them to become hard and thick from calcium deposits. When doctors examine lesions of arterial walls microscopically, they commonly find oxidized fat from free radicals.[19] Any restriction of blood flow to the ear, with a resultant lack of oxygen and nutrients, starves the cells of the inner ear causing them to gradually waste away.

Dozens of scientific studies have shown that cholesterol is an important tissue constituent and a hormone precursor. Therefore, it should never be totally avoided. The real cause of circulatory problems such as arteriosclerosis is not cholesterol, but dietary deficiencies of nutrients that help the body metabolize cholesterol. Chromium, derived from whole food sources (brewer's yeast, sugar beet yeast) provides the body with important cholesterol metabolizing factors. Many researchers consistently point to essential fatty acids as important nutrients for balancing cholesterol and improving circulation.[20-23]

Hydrogenation, homogenization and other processing trends destroy natural fatty acids in foods. How ironic that the food industry offers synthetic fats such as margarine and solid vegetable shortening to replace natural fats. Natural fats need the cholesterol metabolizing factors that synthetic fats take away. In addition, the molecular structure of synthetic fats is different from natural fats and oils, causing them to pile up in the circulatory system. Lacking the essential fatty acids and other natural nutrients, they fail to become metabolized by the human body.

The finest source of essential fatty acids is cold pressed, unrefined and raw green olive oil. Other cold pressed and unrefined raw oils (sunflower, safflower, flaxseed, etc.) also contain fatty acids and should be taken several times a week along with olive oil. A fatty acid deficiency may occur as a result of the processing and refining of foods. My research has clearly shown that fatty acids are critical to the circulatory system of the ear. The ear has the smallest circulatory system of any organ in the body. In some arteries of the inner ear, only one cell can pass through at a time. Fat deposits, bio-unavailable calcium and non-metabolized toxins in the circulatory network of the ear can cause gradual hearing loss.

Fatty acid deficiencies also cause tissue calcium starvation, inner ear congestion, irritation and swelling of various tissues of the body and thyroid problems. Without fatty acids, thyroid hormones do not accomplish their physiological function. In recent years, many scientific studies have demonstrated how important fatty acids are to various systems of the human body.[29-41] Their interaction with calcium and thyroid hormones is critical to cellular health and adequate bone structure and development.

Another common circulatory problem stems from a toxic and alkaline product of protein metabolism called *guanidine*. Guanidine is produced in excess by putrefactive bacteria from undigested protein and glucose. It is often caused by incomplete digestion which, in turn, causes constipation and lower intestinal gas. This toxic substance impairs liver function, inhibiting the removal of toxins from the blood.

Research has shown that when guanidine reaches high levels in the body, it causes calcium and other toxic blood constituents to clog the circulatory system. Two substances can eliminate guanidine from the body. One is acetic acid, found in raw, unpasteurized apple cider vinegar. The other is chlorophyll, which destroys guanidine on contact. Acetic acid combines with guanidine to help eliminate it from the body. Eating raw, uncooked cereal grains provides the liver with inositol and other nutrients. These nutrients allow guanidine and lactic acid to form creatine, which is a useful tissue component. Creatine, in turn, combines with potassium and phosphorus to form an excellent reserve energy source, phosphagen. So, by using natural nutrients you can turn a toxic chemical into an energy source.

Even the heart itself, which pumps blood to the inner ear, de pends upon amino acids, fatty acids, minerals, trace mineral activators, vitamins and enzymes to function optimally. Many researchers have documented how various heart problems are related to nutrient deficiencies and imbalances. For example, complexes of certain B vitamins can improve electrocardiograph readings within only a few minutes after a patient chews them. Sounds incredible! I personally have observed these changes relative to nutrient ingestion. These physiological facts prove that nutrients will improve the efficiency of cardiac function.

In clinical practice, I have observed dramatic changes in blood pressure readings only minutes after a patient was given specific B vitamins (derived from whole food complexes). Low blood pressure is a common finding in people with ear disorders. Restoring normal blood pressure via natural nutrient complexes is critical not only to restore mineral balance, but to provide the ear with optimal circulation. Dietary changes and exercise should always be initiated in combination with food supplements.

Circulation interference also is a problem when people accumulate toxic metals, take drugs and have severe mineral imbalances. For instance, many patients are deficient in phosphorus, fatty acids, and magnesium. As a result, calcium is pulled out of the teeth and bones and into the tissues and circulatory system. Since calcium cannot be utilized, it piles up in joints, muscles, and the circulatory system.

Ginkgo biloba extract is helpful for certain kinds of hearing loss, but not all circulatory problems of the inner ear respond to it. Individuals with poor lymphatic drainage and maldigestion, for example, do not improve with ginkgo biloba. Many cases have allergic reactions and increased fullness and pressure of the inner ear. However, for some individuals, ginkgo biloba has a remarkable ability to increase circulation to the inner ear while improving the availability of the neurotransmittor acetylcholine.[24-26] All medicinal herbs should be used with caution and under medical supervision.

THE ENERGETIC CONNECTION: FUNCTIONAL MEDICINE

The field of Functional Medicine—in which physicians attempt to reestablish homeostatic reintegration and organization of disrupted energy patterns—offers hope for understanding why inner ear disorders occur. During the past decade, I have collected functional-energetic data on hundreds of patients with ear disorders. A long-term analysis of the energetic connections to inner ear disorders revealed the following functional deficits:

- 95% had energy imbalances of the gallbladder meridians.
- 80% had energy imbalances of the small and large intestines.
- 60% had energy imbalances related to dental problems.
- 30% had energy imbalances of the kidney-bladder meridian.
- 25% had energy imbalances of the heart and circulation meridians.
- 20% had energy imbalances of the lymph and sinuses.
- 15% had energy disturbances of the pancreas-spleen meridian.

These findings indicate that functional deficits of the gallbladder are often involved with ear disorders. When the gallbladder is out of balance energetically, it causes secondary disturbances of the intestines, sinuses and kidney-bladder meridians. The gallbladder meridian begins at the outer corner of the eye (GB 1) and travels along the lateral side of the head where several acupoints influence the function of the inner ear. These meridian imbalances make it easy to understand how an imbalance in the gallbladder meridian as it passes through, or in close proximity to, the ears can cause progressive ear disorders.

In my new instructional manual for physicians, *Biological Energetic Regulation Method,* I explain how doctors can balance each meridian with specific doses and potencies of homeopathic remedies. The homeopathic remedies work by radiating a specific vibratory frequency that helps to fine-tune, stabilize and amplify the healing vibrations of the meridians.

The energetic system in the human body is somewhat like an electrical system. The electrical wires are the invisible meridians that give life and energy to all body organs and systems. Before power can be put through a wire, the system must have the correct insulation and resistance. Insufficient insulation and resistance can cause an electrical short circuit or blockage of acupuncture meridians. Since many acupuncture meridians interconnect and interrelate with the hearing process, energetic blockages must be cleared out and harmonized with energetic types of Synchrozyme™ nutrition.*

Synchrozyme™ complexes act synergistically for the body's welfare. This supplementation of enzymes—each with a different profile of activity—is vital to human health and hearing. Its revolutionary process increases the value of nutrients in three important ways:

- Improved absorption
- Increased biological activity
- Enhanced nutrient delivery to cells.

The ear's energy efficiency is dependent on synchronized enzyme reactions that can accomplish the following:

1. They accelerate cellular functions that are too slow and inefficient, as in the case of auditory deficits.
2. They help to renew old and depleted cells.
3. They help to change nutrients into energy and building blocks.
4. They help to remove wastes and by-products of metabolism.
5. They allow vitamins and minerals to perform their vital functions.
6. They protect the cells from free radical damage and enhance immunity.

Many patients—after reading about how zinc or niacin helps to improve hearing and decrease tinnitus—have been disappointed to notice just the opposite effect. This is because they either lack the proper enzymes or the nutrient they took was inorganic and synthetic. The ear has a delicate and subtle balance of enzyme reactions that are easily upset by taking synthetic (USP) vitamins by self-prescription or the generalized recommendations of today's health publications. Taking specific and isolated nutrients may be detrimental to your general health as well.

After over 23 years of investigating different nutritional approaches, I am convinced that there must be a harmonious cooperation of all biological processes. Harmony is only possible in this enzyme-depleted world through the synchronized activity of en-

* Synchrozyme Plus™ is available at fine health food stores everywhere. It is manufactured and distributed by CBE-Synchrozyme, P.O. Box 155, Milford, PA 18337. 717-296-6316.

zymes. All imbalances of the hearing process involve some disruption of our enzymatic balance.

In a recent article for doctors entitled "Biomolecular Nutrition and the Gastrointestinal Tract" (*Townsend Letter for Doctors*, Dec. 1993), I explained how the synchronization of enzymes improved gastrointestinal function in over 400 patients. Using a proprietary blend of complex, enzyme-active nutrients (B vitamins, beta carotene, water soluble organic minerals, fatty acids, amino acids, and gamma-linoleic acid), nutrient absorption and transport and the biomolecular level improved dramatically.

Synchrozyme™ nutrients cannot be analyzed by traditional laboratory methods that are set up to measure USP synthetic vitamins and inorganic minerals or the energetic effects of the synchrozyme process. However, the formulation contains: spirulina, pfaffia paniculata, astragalus, lecithin, royal jelly, antioxidant enzymes (superoxide dismutase, dismutase, catalase), milk thistle, coenzyme Q10, trans ferulic acid, and synchronized enzymes.

Synchrozyme™ nutrients fortify the body on both the physical and energetic level. Each organic nutrient complex radiates a unique and subtle vibration. To assimilate food correctly, a person must absorb the vibrational energy from the food into his/her vital life force. Through this process, the vibrations of synergistic nutrient combinations interact with the multiple oscillating subsystems in the body (vital life force). Most importantly, these vibrating nutrients possess pure harmonic oscillations of energy needed to propel nutrients deep into the cellular environment so they can quickly energize every cell in the body.

The full spectrum of vibrations help to improve the insulation and resistance of the body's electrical circuits by removing meridian-based blockages. The result: meridians that interconnect and interrelate with the hearing process are enhanced.

SELF-HELP AND LIFESTYLE MODIFICATION

THE STRESS CONNECTION

Sensorineural hearing loss and tinnitus have long been a challenge to ear specialists. When a patient reports tinnitus, the question commonly arises as to whether or not it is due to or aggravated by stress.

It is increasingly apparent in today's society that stress is a cause or contributing factor in a virtually unlimited number of health problems. Without exception, nutrient imbalances and a lack of daily exercise can bring on or exaggerate the effects of stress.

Research has shown that we can better cope with the ever increasing demands of today's stressful life by strengthening the body's defenses against stress. When our bodies accumulate too much stress without adaptation, the stress changes into distress reactions that will eventually attack the weakest or most vulnerable organ or body part, which for sufferers of tinnitus, may be the ear.

Many patients with hearing problems commonly report that their hearing and/or tinnitus problem becomes worse when they are under stress. Biofeedback and other relaxation techniques are useful in reducing tension and helping patients successfully adapt to stress. But in order to achieve optimum results, these techniques should be combined with diet, synchronized nutrition and exercise.

Adaptation (or lack of it) is an important factor in all physiological and pathological processes of the inner ear. Hearing-impaired individuals often are caught in a vicious and escalating cycle of stress because of their inability to "listen and relax" during communicative situations. A proper hearing aid that improves the clarity of speech and does not overload the hearing mechanism with excessive loudness can considerably reduce the stress load on a hearing-impaired individual.

LIVING CELL NOURISHMENT

The overprocessing of food, the use of chemical fertilizers combined with the overharvesting of crops have left us with a nutrient-depleted food supply. The majority of today's vitamin supplements don't provide the complex variety of nutrients and enzymes found in whole food sources. In whole, organic foods there are thousands of interrelated organic compounds, all working together in a harmonious way to nourish the cells of our bodies.

As discussed previously, taking isolated "synthetic" vitamins and inorganic minerals can have harmful effects. Multivitamin supplements are not substitutes for whole nourishment. In fact, their pharmaceutical effects cause major imbalances in the body. For every synthetic and inorganic mineral, there is an upper and lower threshold beyond which impairment of immune function can occur. For example, too much magnesium may cause a calcium deficiency, too much sodium may cause a potassium deficiency and too much iron may cause arteriosclerosis. These interactions among nutrients make vitamin and mineral supplementing more complicated than most people realize. Whole food sources contain hundreds of thousands of organic enzyme compounds and nutrients that are still being discovered and studied. Unlike with multivitamins, there is no danger of creating a chemical imbalance or suppressing the immune response—the balance of nutrients is always in harmony with all the systems of the body.

Although the human body can go for long periods of time without food, it can survive only about six minutes without oxygen. Energy production in the muscle cells and almost all the body's vital functions are oxygen-dependent. If the cells do not receive adequate amounts of oxygen, energy occurs only in short bursts without any long-lasting beneficial effects on the body.

Nutritional studies are beginning to suggest that insufficient oxygen is one of the root causes of many degenerative diseases. Diet can determine the oxygen content of our blood. A diet high in refined simple carbohydrates, sugar and fats causes the oxygen delivering red blood cells to stick together, thus limiting the flow of oxygen to the brain and to the rest of the body. This type of diet (followed by the average American) can cut down the oxygen supply by 20 to 30 percent. I believe it is the low oxygen levels in the blood that actually cause the artery walls to become weakened and less resistant to plaque build-up. Megavitamins and most vitamin and mineral formulas with inorganic bonds of minerals also decrease the oxygen content of our blood.

The most important function of nutrients and enzymes is to supply the energy which helps the body perform optimally. The ear is the most energy-needy organ of the body, demanding high quantities of energy-producing nutrients in order to effectively deliver full electrical sound information to the brain. Partial or incomplete nutrient delivery can short-circuit the ear's electrical energy system and result in ear disorders.

Digestion of foods involves a maze of biochemical enzyme reactions, each dependent upon many co-factors and complex forms of nutrients. Digestion entails the breaking down of foods into simpler components so that they may be assimilated in the digestive tract. Many people are unaware of the critical role that digestion plays in the absorption and assimilation of nutrients. Since nutrients reach the cells through the process of digestion, supporting the digestive system with herbs such as ginger, fennel, dandelion and gentian may prove beneficial.

Enzymes are blocked by eating too many acid foods (animal proteins) and by consuming enzyme-dead foods. For example, many studies report hearing and tinnitus improvements when sugar is avoided.[22-29] Other research documents the importance of nutritional and dietary management in hearing disorders.[30-39] My studies have documented the importance of enzymes and biologically active organic nutrient complexes.[40-45]

One of my most recent long-term studies revealed a high incidence of intracellular magnesium deficiency and acid pH of the body. The findings of this comprehensive biochemical study of 14 patients with ear disorders documented that ear symptoms decreased as the biochemistry of the body was brought into balance.[40] Dr. T. Gunther and associates corroborated these findings, reporting magnesium deficiency in patients with nerve-related deafness.[46-51] Other researchers have documented the importance of magnesium to enzymatic function and circulatory health.[52-55] However, the reader must be cautioned not to consume ordinary amino acid chelates of magnesium or other commercially available chelates (gluconate, citrate, aspartate) as these forms of magnesium do not change the intracellular levels of magnesium and in many cases aggravate ear disorders. This study, published in the *Journal of Applied Nutrition*, found that enzyme forms of magnesium (Synchrozyme™ Superfood Complex) resulted in the following clinical findings:

1. Ten out of 17 ears had a decrease in tinnitus intensity and duration.
2. Eight out of 10 reported a decrease in the loudness of tinnitus.
3. All subjects reported relief from ear fullness and loudness sensitivity as well as improved ability to understand speech.

In this groundbreaking, controlled clinical study, I recommended the following dietary goals:

1. Use distilled drinking water.
2. Reduce sodium intake to 250 mg. per day.
3. Reduce intake of acid ash food (meats, grains, etc.) and increase intake of alkaline ash food (fruits, vegetables).
4. Reduce intake of saturated fats, substituting mostly polyunsaturated fats from cold pressed oils and non-animal, high fat proteins (avocado, nuts, coconuts).
5. Eat less animal protein, replacing it with vegetable protein.
6. Eliminate or reduce intake of processed and refined sugars.
7. Increase consumption of complex carbohydrates and naturally occurring sugars in fruits and vegetables.
8. Reduce intake of high phosphorus foods by 20 to 50 percent (meats, grains).
9. Increase intake of whole foods in their raw, natural state (fresh fruits, vegetables, nuts, seeds).
10. A daily intake of Synchrozyme™ nutrition

THE IMPORTANCE OF DIET

Long-term consumption of acid foods decreases the body's energy and suppresses immunity, while long-term ingestion of alkaline foods nourishes and revitalizes. My scientific research and extensive clinical case files show that most symptoms decrease as the pH becomes more alkaline and overall health improves.

The pH (acid and alkaline balance) of the food must be compatible with the body's pH which is 80 percent alkaline and 20 percent acid by design. Most diets, even vegetarian diets, are 75 percent acid and 25 percent alkaline.

Excess acidity depletes alkaline minerals and blocks enzymes which are critical for cellular health and the optimal efficiency of organs and glands. It often results in a lack of stomach hydrochloric acid: acid, instead of alkaline bile, completely inactivates all pancreatic enzymes (which research by physiologists has shown to be optimal only at an alkaline 8.0 pH). The inactivation of these pancreatic enzymes results in poor assimilation of nutrients and a high infiltration of toxins into the blood and lymph systems. This is due to undigested food which is fermenting, rotting and becoming putrid as it passes through over 40 feet of the intestinal tract. During the first few months on my diet program it may be necessary to energize the digestive system with fresh herbs such as ginger, peppermint and fennel to help improve the digestion and absorption of nutrients.

The nutritional value of food is dependent upon the following factors:

1. The wholeness of the food. Foods from nature are preferable to man-made or processed food. Foods as close to a natural state as possible, not overcooked or processed, are the best choice.

2. The living qualities (enzyme content) of food. Enzymes are found in abundance in raw food and are easily destroyed by cooking and processing techniques.

3. The ash (alkaline or acid) quality of foods. Alkaline foods are preferable to acidic foods, and should make up 75 percent of one's diet. Most fruits and vegetables are alkaline, while most animal-derived protein and grains are acidic.

4. The quantity of the food. Even too much good quality food can overload the digestive system, causing excess energy consumption and excessive internal stress from maldigestion. A good rule: Never eat more food than can be held in two hands at one meal.

Additional Dietary Guidelines

1. Food combining:
   A. Do not eat proteins (flesh, dairy, eggs, nuts, seeds and legumes) with starches (grains, potatoes, beans).
   B. Do not eat fruits with vegetables or starches.
   C. Do not eat citrus fruits, strawberries and pineapple with sweet fruits (dates, banana, all dried fruits, carob).
   D. Eat melons alone.
2. Do not eat dessert after a meal. Wait at least two hours, then eat a healthy dessert.
3. Do not drink excessively with meals. Too many fluids after or during meals suppress enzyme activity and digestion.
4. Eat slowly and chew food well. Try to eat when you are relaxed.
5. Those with weak digestive systems should soak all nuts and seeds overnight before consumption.
6. Try to eat more alkaline foods with each meal. A raw salad with an oil and lemon-type herbal dressing is the best way to get these alkaline foods in your diet. Eating fresh fruits between meals also helps to make the body alkaline.
7. Decrease or eliminate your daily intake of high acid-forming foods (seafood, poultry, meats, eggs, dairy) and eat only about 25-50 percent of low acid-forming foods (whole grains, nuts, seeds).

Those who want to see how well this diet program works should keep a personal health diary for a month or two, recording daily how they feel, look, sleep, and wake up, plus their energy level, regularity, and disposition. Keeping a daily diary prevents discouragement because improvements will occur in the functional capacity of the body long before improvements occur at the ear level. In addition, a health diary is a good way to get in touch with your body and monitor your progress. Most of these health related changes are subtle and occur so slowly that most people are unaware of them.

People who follow this diet typically report they have more energy, and sleep more soundly, and they notice that their finger nails have become stronger with a healthy, pink color beneath the nail bed. These changes reflect better metabolism and circulation and are indications of better health.

Adequate aerobic exercise along with proper diet will increase an individual's supply of oxygen while at the same time reducing stress.

When people exercise, they oxygenate themselves. Exercise is one of the most valuable and important balancers of bodily functions.

TAKING RESPONSIBILITY

Self-help means taking responsibility for your health habits, environment and lifestyle. Individuals must reclaim personal control over their lives in order to get relief from ear disorders.

In summary, the energy available for chemical, osmotic or electrical work in the sound transmission of the inner ear must be balanced between supply and demand of energy-producing nutrients in order to prevent serious impairment of the inner ear. Energy-depleted hair cells of the inner ear can be restored to more efficient performance when nutrition is optimal. The ideal consideration for insuring proper ear function is to ingest a continuous, healthy supply of whole food nutrient complexes.

Stopping and reversing hearing problems involves not only the right attitude but a willingness to learn more about healthy lifestyle changes. This information is presented to help individuals appreciate the importance of balance in the human body achieved with whole nourishment from enzymatic complexes of nutrients.

Once an individual decides to accept the responsibility for his or her health—by making basic lifestyle changes—then improved health and hearing can be a reality.

REFERENCES

1. Kardinaal, A.F.M., et al. "Antioxidants in adipose tissue and risk of myocardial infarction: The EURAMIC study." *The Lancet* 352 (8884):1379–1384, Dec. 4, 1993.
2. Rimm, Eric B., Sc.D., Stampfer, Meir J., M.D., et al. "Vitamin E consumption and the risk of coronary heart disease in men." *The New England Journal of Medicine* 328(20):1450–1456, 1993.
3. Warner, Huber R. "Overview mechanisms of antioxidant action on

life span." In *Antioxidants: Chemical, Physiological, Nutritional and Toxicological Aspects,* American Health Foundation Food and Nutrition Council and Environmental Health and Safety Council, Gary M. Williams, ed. in chief. Princeton, N.J.: Princeton Scientific, 1993, 151–61.

4. Passwater, Richard A. *The Antioxidants: The Nutrients That Guard Us Against Cancer, Heart Disease, Arthritis, and Allergies—and Even Slow the Aging Process.* New Canaan, Conn.: Keats, 1985, p. 19.

5. Levine, Stephen A., Kidd, Parris M. "Antioxidant adaptation: A unified disease theory." Reprinted from *Journal of Orthomolecular Psychiatry* 14:1, 33 (p. 15 of reprint) (hereafter cited as "A unified disease theory") 1984.

6. Bretlau, P., et al. "Otospongiosis and sodium fluoride. A clinical double-blind, placebo-controlled study on sodium fluoride treatment in otospongiosis." *Am J Otol* 10(1):20–22, 1989.

7. Colletti, V., Fiorino, F.G. "Stapedius reflex in the monitoring of NaF treatment of subclinical otosclerosis." *Acta Otolaryngol (Stockh)* 104(5-6):447–53, 1987.

8. Forquer, B.D., et al. "Sodium fluoride: Effectiveness of treatment for cochlear otosclerosis." *Am J Otol* 7(2):121–25, 1986.

9. Carrillo, V., et al. "Disorders of glucose tolerance and pathology of the labyrinth." *Acta Otorhinolaryngol Belg* 38(5):474–84, 1984 (in French).

10. Proctor, B., Proctor, C. "Metabolic management in Menière's disease." *Ann Otolrhinolaryngol* 90(6 Pt 1):615–18, 1981.

11. Sikora, M.A., et al. "Diet-induced hyperlipidemia and auditory dysfunction." *Acta Otolaryngol (Stockh)* 102(5-6):372–81, 1986.

12. Pillsbury, H.C. "Hypertension, hyperlipoproteinemia, chronic noise exposure: Is there synergism in cochlear pathology?" *Laryngoscope* 96(10):1112–38, 1986.

13. Gosselin, E.J., Yanick, P., Jr. "Audiologic and metabolic findings in 90 patients with fluctuant hearing loss." *J Am Audiol Soc* 2(1):15–18, 1976.

14. Spencer, J.T., Jr. "Hyperlipoproteinemia and inner ear disease." *J Int Acad Metabology* 4:38–42, 1975.

15. Browning, G.G., et al. "Blood viscosity as a factor in sensorineural hearing impairment." *The Lancet* 1:121–23, 1986.

16. Strome, M., et al. "Hyperlipidemia in association with childhood sensorineural hearing loss." *Laryngoscope* 98(2):165–9, 1988.

17. Spencer, J.T., Jr. "Hyperlipoproteinemia, hyperinsulinism and Menière's disease." *South Med J* 74:1194–97, 1981.

18. Rosen, S., et al. "Dietary prevention of hearing loss." *Acta Otolaryngol (Stockh)* 70(4):242–47, 1970.

19. Diplock, Anthony T. "Antioxidant nutrients and disease prevention: An overview." Supplement to the *American Journal of Clinical Nutrition* 53:1, January 1991, 190S.

20. Murphy, R.C., Mathews, R., Picket, W. "Leukotrienes and thromboxanes: metabolites of essential fatty acids with significant untoward pharmacological properties." In *Nutritional Factors: Modulating Effects*

on *Metabolic Processes*, Beers, R.F., Jr., Bassett, E.G., eds. New York: Raven Press, 1981, pp. 495–510.
21. Goodnight, S.H., Harris, W.S., Connor, W.E., et al. "Polyunsaturated fatty acids, hyperlipidemia and thrombosis." *Arteriosclerosis* 2:87–113, 1982.
22. Horrobin, D.F. "The regulation of prostaglandin biosynthesis: Negative feedback mechanisms and the selective formation of 1 and 2 series prostaglandins: Relevance to inflammation and immunity." *Med Hypotheses* 6:687–709, 1980.
23. Holman, Ralph T. "Effect of dietary trans fatty acids upon prostaglandin precursors." In *Nutritional Factors: Modulating Effects on Metabolic Processes*, Beers, R. F. Jr., Bassett, E.G., eds. New York: Raven Press, 1981, pp. 523–538.
24. Drieu, K. "Multiplicity of effects of ginkgo biloba extract: Current status and new trends." In *Effects of Ginkgo Biloba Extracts on Organic Cerebral Impairment*. Eurotext Ltd., 1985.
25. Kleijnen, J., and Knipschild, P. "Ginkgo biloba." *The Lancet* 340(7):1136–1139, 1992.
26. Taillandier, J., et al. "Ginkgo biloba extract in the treatment of cerebral disorders due to aging." In *Rokan (Ginkgo Biloba), Recent Results in Pharmacology and Clinic*, E.W. Funfgeld, ed. Berlin: Springer-Verlag, 1988.
27. Spencer, J.T., Jr. "Hyperlipoproteinemia, hyperinsulinism and Menière's disease." *South Med J* 74:1194–97, 1981.
28. Weille, F.R. "Hypoglycemia in Menière's disease." *Arch Otol* 87:129, 1968.
29. Lohle, E. "The influence of chronic vitamin A deficiency on human and animal ears." *Arch Otorhinolaryngol* 234:167–73, 1982.
30. Yanick, P. "Nutritional aspects of tinnitus and hearing disorders." In *Tinnitus and its Management*, Yanick, P., Jr., Clark, J.G., eds. Springfield, Illinois: Charles C. Thomas, 1984.
31. Yanick, P. "Solving problematic tinnitus: A clinical scientific approach." *Townsend Letter for Doctors*, February-March, 1985, p. 31.
32. Lohle, E. "The influence of chronic vitamin A deficiency on human and animal ears." *Arch Otorhinolaryngol* 234:167–73, 1982.
33. Lobel, M.J. "Is hearing loss due to nutritional deficiency?" *Arch Otolaryngol* May, 1951, 515–26.
34. Romeo, G. "The therapeutic effect of vitamins A and E in neurosensory hearing loss." *Acta Vitaminol Enzymol* 7 Suppl:85–92, 1985.
35. Ikeda, K., et al. "The effect of vitamin D deficiency on the cochlear potentials and the perilymphatic ionized calcium concentration of rats." *Acta Otolaryngol Suppl (Stockh)* 435:64–72, 1987.
36. Brookes, G.B. "Vitamin D deficiency and otosclerosis." *Otolaryngol Head Neck Surg* 93(3):313–21, 1985.
37. Brookes, G.B. "Vitamin D deficiency—A new cause of cochlear deafness." *J Laryngol Otol* 97(5):405–20, 1983.
38. Meyer zum Gottesberge AM. "Imbalanced calcium homeostasis and

indolymphatic hydrops." *Acta Otolaryngol Suppl (Stockh)* 460:18–27, 1988.

39. Ikeda, K., et al. "The effect of vitamin D deficiency on the cochlear potentials and the perilymphatic ionized calcium concentration of rats." *Acta Otolaryngol Suppl (Stockh)* 435:64–72, 1987.

40. Yanick, P., Jr. "Dietary and lifestyle influences on cochlear disorders and biochemical status: a 12-month study." *J Appl Nutr* 40(2):75–84, 1988.

41. Yanick, P., Jr. *Rehabilitation strategies for sensorineural hearing loss.* (Editor and Contributing Author) published by Grune and Stratton, 1979.

42. Yanick, P., Jr. "Tinnitus: A holistic approach." *Hearing Instruments* 32:12–15, 1981.

43. Yanick, P., Jr. "New hope for hearing and tinnitus problems: Nutrition and biochemistry." *Hearing Instruments,* 32:12–15, 1981.

44. Yanick, P. Jr. *You Can Feel Better.* Woodbridge, New Jersey: Sunshine Press, 1982.

45. Yanick, P., Jr. "Nutritional aspects of tinnitus and hearing disorders." In *Tinnitus and its Management,* by Yanick, P., Clark, J.G., eds. Springfield, Illinois: Charles C. Thomas, 1984.

46. Gunther, T., Ising, H., Merker, H.J. "Elekrtolyt- und kollagengehalf im rattenherzen bei chronischem magnesium-mangel und stress." *J Clin Chem Clin Biochem* 16:293, 1978.

47. Gunther, T. "Biochemistry and pathobiochemistry of magnesium." *Magnesium-Bulletin* 1a:91, 1981.

48. Ising, H., Gunther, T., Melchert, H.U. "Nachweis und wirkungsmechanismen der blutdrucksteigernden wirkung von arbeitslarm." *Zbl. Arbaeitsmed* 30:194, 1980.

49. Ising, H. Gunther, T., Handrock, M., Michalak, R., Schwarze, J., Vormann, J., Wuster, G.A. "Magnesium and larmwirkungen." *Magnesium-Bulletin* 1a:155, 1981.

50. Ising, H., Handrock, M., Gunther, T., Fischer, R., Dombrowski, M "Increased noise trauma in guinea pigs through magnesium deficiency." *Arch Otorhinolaryng* 236:139, 1982.

51. Joachims, Z., Babisch, W., Ising, H., Gunther, T., Handrock, M. "Dependence of noise-induced hearing loss upon perilymph magnesium concentration." *J Acoust Soc Amer,* 1983.

52. Aikawa, J.K. *Magnesium: Its Biological Significance.* Boca Raton, Florida CRC Press, 1981.

53. Lehr, D., Blaiklock, R., Brown, A. "Magnesium loss as a reliable measure of acute myocardial injury." In *Magnesium in Health and Disease* Cantin, Seelig. Holliswood: Spectrum Publications, 1980, pp. 499–506

54. Hudspeth, A.J. "The cellular basis of hearing: The biophysics of hair cells." *Science* 230:745–752, 1985.

55. Altura, B.M., Altura, B.T. "Magnesium-calcium interactions and con traction of arterial smooth muscle in ischemic heart diseases, hyper tension and vasospastic disorders." In Wester, *Electrolytes and th Heart.* New York: Trans Medica, 1983, pp. 41–56.